CONTACT:

Instagram: @mahoganywritez

Facebook: Mahogany Clark

Twitter: @mahoganywritez

Email: borntosoar81@gmail.com

Hello. I am Mahogany Clark, and I will be informing you of four types of ways that you can market your book: visually, personally, and socially, and through your brand. Thank you for investing in me; I do believe my tips will help you.

Visually

- Videos

- Live videos

- Clothing

- Promotional flyer

Videos

Videos give your audience a visual

understanding of what you are marketing.

People are more likely to stop and look at a

video than pay attention to text. Make sure that

your videos are high-quality, have great lighting,

and are straight to the point. This means your

videos should be thirty seconds to one minute

long.

Live Videos

Live videos are a great way to market your book, because you can do live reading snippets. This is an example of how you can give exclusives to your audience in real time. You can even answer questions your audience may have about your book/product.

Clothing & Promotional flyers

Creating T-shirts, jackets, hats, and pants that showcase your brand is a very creative way to market. Just imagine walking around with your book cover, title, and/or logo on your clothing so everyone can see. You may get stopped by people asking questions, or they may just search your product. If you get stopped by people, it will be an excellent way for you to sell your book/product in person! Flyers are great for promotional purposes. I use an app called Flyer Maker to create my promotional flyers. The templates are ready-made, and all you have to do is edit and share!

Personally

- Pictures

- Giveaways

- Team-building

- Mentors

Pictures & Giveaways

Personal pictures with your audience and/or pictures of your audience with your book/product give you more credibility. The more people see others with your book/product, the more they will want to purchase it! Giveaways help you give back to your supporters; people love to know that they are appreciated. This helps you get closer and appear more relatable to your audience.

Team-building & mentors

Team-building is extremely important. It will help you in the long run, both when you are launching your book/product and when your book/product is released. Your team will support you by purchasing your book/product, being reliable, and helping you create buzz. This team can consist of 10-20 people; however, the more the better! Mentors will help you by giving their critique and expertise. Finding someone who is in the same field as you are will not only help you get ahead but will help you make decisions and be the best at your craft.

Socially

- Collaboration

- Support

- Being active/interactive

- Vending events

- Multiple social media pages

- Promotion

Collaboration & Support

Collaborating with and supporting people will take you a very long way on your journey! For example, I did a book signing with another author that I met locally, and we ended up building a more personal relationship. Now, when either of us know of anything that can help the other, we share it with the other person. When it comes to supporting, I make sure I support others' products for no charge at all. In fact, I support their work as if it were my own, whether sharing or purchasing. You never know what can happen. You show support as you would want someone to support you.

Also, people who have platforms such as radio stations, podcasts, magazines, and social groups can help with exposure. I literally booked my own radio/podcast interviews for FREE! Facebook has so many groups for authors/entrepreneurs. All you have to do is ask to be on these individuals' platforms; they are looking for people like you. I have paid small fees to be in magazines and have received offers to be in magazines. I have also been offered radio interviews. When people see you working hard, they are sometimes willing to reward you! I have even landed interviews on the Roku Channel on TV, twice.

Here is a list of radio stations/podcasts/other

platforms I have been interviewed on. You can contact them to get on their platform for no cost!

24/7 CEO - Spotlight Thursday

AMG Entertainment Network - This interview, also available on the ROKU CHANNEL, was my very first TV interview with Bruce Glasgow and Michael Neely Yaya Diamond - Dare to Be Different

Crazy Train Radio - Radio Show Blackgirlswrite2 - Author Zoom Calls

Cheap Pops Radio - Radio Show TalkTruth Series - Podcast Show GiveASisterAHug - The Journey of Relationships Podcast

Jacksonsproduction - living the dream with

curveball

Podcast Show

Soul Forge Podcast - Podcast Show

Alecia Wilson - The Social Bar Podcast Show

The Sunday Night Army - Podcast Show

Nigel Beckles - Nigel Beckles Podcast

The JusB Show - Podcast Show with JusB

Bradley

Sharifah Hardie - The Round Table Podcast

Leaders

Recognizing Leaders – Interview

Romelia Lungu (Author) - Blog Interview

Queenie Clem - Blog Interview

Hezekiah Morris - Drip Da Mic Show

Shonta Gibson (Tyrese's Gibson sister) - Queen

G Live

Experience!! This is live on the Roku Channel! I

am also currently taking her Authors Course, as

well. Authors Spotlight - Zoë Davis Live readings

- Libra J Hicks ReplyForward

Being active/Interactive

Being active is very important. This means posting consistently and/or on a daily basis. People need to see you on their timeline promoting as much as possible. Sometimes people don't always purchase the first time they see a post, but if they see you enough, it will pique their interest. Interacting with your people is very important, as well. People love feedback from the person that they support. You can't always get to everyone, but it means a lot when you make the effort to get to most!

Vending Events

Vending events are a great way to get yourself out there in the community. Not only will you meet people that are like-minded, but people from your community will see you. This will help you gain exposure. You can get those personal photos and have those up-close conversations with your audience/supporters! This is where I personally connect with my supporters. If your community has food truck pop ups and/or pop-up shops, please do not hesitate to sign up and participate!

Multiple Social Media Pages

I have two Facebook accounts, three Instagram

pages, one Twitter account, and one Snapchat!

The more social pages that you have, the more

you can share all at once.

Every time I share something, I post on every

account and every page each time! Now, you

can focus on building one page specifically, but

it does not hurt to have plenty—it only helps.

Promotion

Promo, for short, will also help with your exposure. However, you cannot have just anyone promote your book/product, because you want to get your money's worth! So let's say you are an author but you are following another author who has a larger platform. Reaching out to them via email, DM, and/or phone for promotion will make the most sense. Influencers with a larger following are trusted individuals, and they have status and credentials with a larger audience. If they tell someone to check out your book, it will bring attention

to your page, followers, and most

importantly, sales!

Branding

- Business cards

- Bookmarks

- Posters

- Notebooks

- Pins

- Flyers

- Banners

- Tablecloths

- Logo

Branding

Business cards, bookmarks, posters, notebooks, pins, flyers, banners, logos and tablecloths, all with your book/product on them, is branding yourself! This is establishing your brand—what it represents, its uniqueness—and capturing attention! Also, the more variety you have in your brand, the more people can see that you are passionate about your craft and that you care to give your supporters more variety! Just think: Every book has a cover, and every business has a logo.

Now that you have learned four major ways to market your book/product, don't wait to make it successful! Thank you, and happy success!